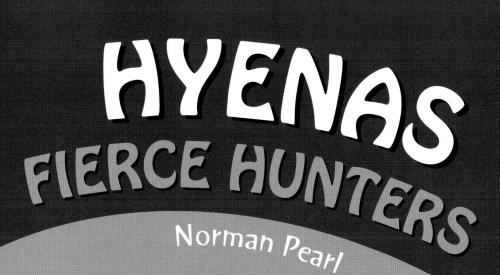

HYENAS
FIERCE HUNTERS

Norman Pearl

PowerKiDS press.

New York

Published in 2009 by The Rosen Publishing Group, Inc.
29 East 21st Street, New York, NY 10010

First Edition

Editor: Amelie von Zumbusch
Book Design: Julio Gil
Photo Researcher: Jessica Gerweck

Photo Credits: Cover, pp. 7, 9, 15, 17, 19 Shutterstock.com; p. 5 © www.iStockphoto.com/Elvis Santana; p. 11 © Michel & Christine Denis-Huot/BIOS/Peter Arnold, Inc.; p. 13 © Craig Lang; p. 21 © Suzi Eszterhas/Getty Images; back cover (top to bottom) Shutterstock.com, Shutterstock.com, © Kim Wolhuter/Getty Images, Shutterstock.com, © Stephen Frink/Getty Images, Shutterstock.com.

Library of Congress Cataloging-in-Publication Data

Pearl, Norman.
  Hyenas : fierce hunters / Norman Pearl. — 1st ed.
      p. cm. — (Powerful predators)
  Includes index.
  ISBN 978-1-4042-4508-2 (library binding)
  1. Hyenas—Juvenile literature. I. Title.
  QL737.C24.P43 2009
  599.74'3—dc22
                                          2008006839

Manufactured in the United States of America

Contents

But It Looks Like a Dog!

Hyenas are unusual animals that live in Asia and Africa. Though they look a bit like dogs, hyenas are really more closely related to cats. As cats and dogs are, hyenas are smart predators, or hunters. In fact, hyenas are so successful that they have been around for 24 million years.

Over time, people have told strange stories about hyenas. Some said that hyenas had magical powers. People even thought that witches rode on the backs of hyenas! None of these stories are true, though. Hyenas are just animals that can seem scary because we do not know a lot about them.

Many people do not know that hyenas are skilled predators, or hunters.

Where the Hyenas Are

There are three kinds of hyenas. These are striped hyenas, spotted hyenas, and brown hyenas. The striped hyena is found in Africa, the Middle East, and Asia. It often lives in dry, rocky places with low-growing plants.

Spotted hyenas and brown hyenas are both found only in Africa. The spotted hyena lives in eastern, western, and southern Africa. This hyena often lives on flat, grassy plains with few trees called savannas. Spotted hyenas are also found at the edges of **tropical rain forests**. Brown hyenas live throughout southern Africa. They are found in both deserts and savannas.

This spotted hyena's coat makes the animal hard to see against the grasses of the savanna where it lives.

A Strange-Looking Animal

All hyenas have wide heads, powerful **jaws**, and lots of teeth. Spotted hyenas are about the size of an adult German shepherd dog. Brown hyenas and striped hyenas are smaller. All hyenas have front legs that are longer than their back legs. This makes hyenas seem to **limp** when they walk. However, hyenas can walk well and run very fast.

Hyenas also have short manes of hair on their backs. When a hyena is **excited**, the animal's mane stands up. This makes the hyena look much bigger than it is, which is useful in scaring off enemies.

Striped hyenas, such as this animal, and brown hyenas have pointed ears.
Spotted hyenas have more rounded ears. All hyenas have excellent hearing.

Hyena Clans

For years, people thought that hyenas lived alone. However, we now know that most hyenas live in groups, called clans. There can be as many as 100 animals in a spotted hyena clan. Brown hyena clans are smaller, with just 4 to 15 animals in them. Striped hyenas generally live alone or in small family groups.

The members of a hyena clan live together in the **territory** the clan has marked off. In striped and spotted hyena clans, the **females** are in charge! They are **dominant** over the **males**. In brown hyena clans, certain females are equal to males and sometimes get into fights with them.

Spotted hyenas generally share their food with other members of their clans. Often, dozens of spotted hyenas feed on just one animal.

A Hyena's Life

Hyena clans have dens within their territories. Young hyenas live in these dens. Adult hyenas generally gather around a den instead of staying inside it. Hyena dens are often caves or holes dug into hillsides. Sometimes, hyenas use the empty dens of other animals.

Some hyena homes can be very noisy. People often say that someone laughs like a hyena. This is because many people think the sound spotted hyenas make when they are scared is like wild laughter. Spotted hyenas also make "whooping" noises to bring their clans together for a hunt or a fight. Striped and brown hyenas are quieter.

Hyenas do not keep their dens very clean. The land around a hyena den is often covered with the bones of animals the hyenas have eaten.

Here Come the Hyena Cubs!

Hyena babies are called cubs. Mother hyenas generally have between two and four cubs in a litter, or at one time. Brown and striped hyena cubs are born sightless and helpless. However, spotted hyenas are born with their eyes open and are quickly ready for action.

Sometimes, spotted hyena cubs even fight one another soon after they are born. The fighting is often worst between two spotted female hyena cubs from the same litter. At times, the stronger cub kills the weaker one.

Each hyena makes its own special sounds. Spotted hyena
mothers and babies recognize each other by these sounds.

Growing Up as a Hyena

A few weeks after their babies are born, spotted hyena mothers bring the young cubs to the large clan den. There, the hyena mothers nurse, or feed their milk to, their young until the cubs can hunt for themselves. Sometimes, these hyena cubs nurse for as long as a year and a half. During that time, they learn to hunt. Then, they are ready to live on their own.

Brown hyena cubs live in clan dens, too. In fact, adult brown hyenas will even feed and care for the cubs of other clan members. Striped hyenas often use caves as dens. Mother and father striped hyenas both bring food to their young.

When they grow up, young female hyenas will stay in their mothers'
clans, while male hyenas will generally become part of another clan.

Strong Predators

Once they have learned to hunt, hyenas can feed themselves quite well. They are powerful hunters. Brown hyenas and striped hyenas generally hunt alone. Spotted hyenas often hunt in packs to chase down large **prey**. These animals are good runners and can run up to 34 miles per hour (55 km/h). Once their prey tires, the hyenas pull the prey down and **disembowel** it. A spotted hyena's jaws and teeth are among the strongest in the animal world!

Spotted hyenas often take on prey three times their size, such as zebras, wildebeests, young giraffes, and water buffalo. Striped hyenas and brown hyenas generally eat smaller animals.

Brown hyenas, such as this one, eat mostly meat. These hyenas also sometimes eat fruit. Striped hyenas have been known to eat fruit, as well.

Feeding Time

At times, spotted hyenas steal food from smaller predators, such as wild dogs and cheetahs. However, bigger predators, such as lions, steal kills from hyenas, too. Sometimes, after killing a large animal, hyenas do not even get to eat their prey. A lion comes along and takes it from them instead. Lions also prey on hyenas.

All hyenas are scavengers as well as hunters. That means that hyenas eat carrion, or the remains of animals that have been dead for some time. A hyena's strong jaws help it **crush** the bones, teeth, and other leftover parts of a kill.

These spotted hyenas are scavenging the remains of
another animal's kill on the Masai Mara, a park in Kenya.

Just Animals

Many people dislike hyenas. At times, these animals have **attacked** and killed both adults and children. Some people think **tombstones** were first used in the Middle East to stop hyenas from digging up **graves** and eating the bodies in them.

Yet people have hurt hyenas, too. Farmers often kill hyenas that have eaten farm animals. People also kill hyenas to gather certain body parts they think can be used for medicine, or drugs. Today, though, people are learning to respect hyenas. Hyenas are not bad animals or mean killers. They are just predators trying to live another day in their world.

Glossary

attacked (uh-TAKD) Started a fight with.

crush (KRUSH) To destroy something by pressing.

disembowel (dis-em-BOW-el) To rip the insides out of something.

dominant (DAH-mih-nent) In charge.

excited (ik-SY-ted) Stirred up.

females (FEE-maylz) Women and girls.

graves (GRAYVZ) Places where dead people are buried.

jaws (JAHZ) Bones in the top and bottom of the mouth.

limp (LIMP) To walk or run unevenly.

males (MAYLZ) Men and boys.

prey (PRAY) An animal that is hunted by another animal for food.

territory (TER-uh-tor-ee) Land or space that animals guard for their use.

tombstones (TOOM-stohnz) Stones marking where dead people are buried.

tropical rain forests (TRAH-puh-kul RAYN FOR-ests) Warm, wet forests
located in the warmest parts of Earth.

Index

A
Africa, 4, 6
Asia, 4, 6

B
backs, 4, 8
brown hyenas, 6, 8, 12, 18

D
dogs, 4, 20

F
females, 10

G
graves, 22

J
jaws, 8, 18, 20

M
males, 10
manes, 8
Middle East, 6, 22

P
plains, 6
prey, 18, 20

S
spotted hyenas, 6, 8, 12, 14, 18, 20
striped hyenas, 6, 8, 10, 12, 16, 18

T
territories, 10, 12
tombstones, 22
trees, 6
tropical rain forests, 6

W
witches, 4

Web Sites

Due to the changing nature of Internet links, PowerKids Press has developed an online list of Web sites related to the subject of this book. This site is updated regularly. Please use this link to access the list:
www.powerkidslinks.com/pred/hyena/